Easy-To-Tell
Stories for Young Children

Easy-To-Tell
Stories for Young Children

Annette Harrison

NATIONAL STORYTELLING PRESS

Jonesborough, Tennessee

Published by the National Storytelling Press
of the National Storytelling Association
P.O. Box 309 ■ Jonesborough, Tenn. 37659 ■ 615-753-2171

Printed in the United States

Edited by Mary C. Weaver
Interior design by Jane L. Hillhouse
Cover design by Willowisp Press
Photographs by Tom Raymond, Fresh Air Photographics

The story "Bobbie the Boo" is adapted from *Yetta the Trickster* by Andrea
Griffing Zimmerman. Copyright © 1976 by Andrea Griffing Zimmerman.
Reprinted by permission of Clarion Books/Houghton Mifflin Company. All
rights reserved.

Library of Congress Cataloging-in-Publication Data
Harrison, Annette, 1941–
   Easy-to-Tell Stories for Young Children/Annette Harrison.
     p. cm.
   ISBN 1-879991-12-8: $8.95
    1. Storytelling. 2. Education, Elementary. 3. Teaching—Aids and devices.
I. Title.
LB1042.H38 1992   92-29827
372.64'2—dc20   CIP

To Andy and Fred

With special thanks to

Ruthilde Kronberg, for her creative and loving
assistance with the stories

Lynn Rubright, for being my mentor and a caring friend

Sheila Onuska, for her help in shaping this manuscript

Jon Pingree, for his clerical assistance and
willingness to meet deadlines.

Contents

Introduction

Most young children are loving, open, joyful creatures, and when I tell stories to them, I always get back more than I give. Just for sharing stories, I see expressive, happy faces, and eyes full of wonder. I hear voices chanting a chorus of song or giggling, barking, meowing, and clucking in unison with me. Together we create a joyful storytelling experience.

The young child often lives in the world of make-believe, so he or she slips easily into the narrated story. The child readily identifies with the characters, experiences the adventure, and absorbs the meaning. Children intuitively know that the story can help them learn about themselves and understand the world around them. Stories encourage the development of feelings and empathy and speak to the inner child. Stories are heard by the brain but felt by the heart. The children always ask for more.

With all of this in mind, I've put together this collection of 12 easy-to-tell stories adapted specifically for use with young listeners. These multicultural stories have simple plots, strong and interesting characters, quick action, and satisfying resolution. They are filled with the wisdom of folklore. In folklore good and evil are unmistakable, and the stories make very clear that our behavior has consequences. So the stories teach and entertain at the same time.

This collection contains adaptations of such familiar stories as "The Three Billy Goats Gruff," "Anansi the Spider," and "Johnny Appleseed" as well as a sprinkling of well-known fables. I have also created some new stories from old folkloric themes, just for this book.

On the page preceding each story, I've indicated its source and given some suggestions for when and how to tell it. Keep in mind that all of these stories can be told at any time. Running alongside the text of each story are additional instructions on ways to use your voice, facial expressions, and gestures to enhance the dramatic value of the tale. Of course, these are only suggestions, to be used as needed. Once you begin telling stories, you'll find that your own gestures flow naturally from you. So relax, use what feels comfortable, and make the story yours.

Don't feel that you need to memorize the stories. Read them a number of times, learn the verses and songs if you choose to use them, and then tell the stories. Visualizing a story's events as they unfold will help you remember them. Practice the story out loud, finding its rhythm and discovering expressive ways to use your voice. The more you practice, the more confident you'll become.

Take these stories, make them your own, and share them. Your audience awaits!

The Three Butterfly Brothers

Source:
A German folk tale, adapted.

When to tell:
■ To introduce the spring.
■ To teach acceptance of one another and our differences.
■ To teach or reinforce color recognition.

Suggestions:
■ Show pictures of butterflies.
■ Let the children play the butterflies in the story. Teach them to make their hands into butterflies or to flap their arms like wings.
■ Find a red, a yellow, and a white object in the room, and hold each one up at appropriate times during the telling.

The Three Butterfly Brothers

Once there were three butterfly brothers: Butterfly Red, Butterfly White, and Butterfly Yellow.

One beautiful spring day when the birds were singing and the bees were buzzing, the three brothers decided to go to the garden to visit the flowers.

They flew from flower to flower to flower.

They were having a wonderful time, when suddenly it began to rain: *splish splash, splish splash.*

"Oh no! It's raining, and my wings are getting wet!" said Butterfly Red.

"Mine too," said Butterfly White. "Let's go home."

"I'll lead the way," said Butterfly Yellow. "Follow me."

The rain kept coming down: *splish splash, splish splash.*

The three butterfly brothers flew all the way home, but when they got there, the door was closed. They took hold of the doorknob and pulled and pulled and pulled!

"It's locked!" said Butterfly Red. "What will we do?"

"I know," said Butterfly Yellow. "We'll fly back to the garden and ask the flowers to open up their cups so that we can fly inside. Then they'll close their flower cups, and we'll be safe and dry."

And the rain came down: *splish splash, splish splash.*

"I'll lead the way," said Butterfly White. "Hurry, hurry!"

They flew all the way back to the garden. They were

Hold up the appropriately colored objects.

Chirp together, and buzz together.

Fly together in place.

Make the rain sound with your hands on your knees, alternating one hand and the other.

Each time you mention a butterfly's color, hold up the appropriate object, and let the children say the color's name with you.

Fly with the children; if the group is small, fly around the room and back.

Have the children join you in making pulling movements.

Demonstrate this with your hands.

Now say splish splash *faster and faster each time the words appear.*

Fly together.

getting wetter and wetter, and their wings were getting heavier and heavier.

"Look!" said Butterfly Yellow. "There's a red and yellow tulip. Let's ask her to protect us from the rain."

"Oh, little red and yellow tulip, please open up your cup for us to protect us from the rain."

Fly up to one of the children, perhaps one wearing red or yellow clothing.

Save us, save us
From the rain
Until the sun
Comes out again.

Say the verse once, and have the children repeat it with you.

The tulip answered, "Butterfly Red and Butterfly Yellow can come in because they are just like me—but not Butterfly White. He is different!"

"Well," answered the red and yellow butterflies, "then we don't want to come in either. We love our brother Butterfly White, and we won't leave him out in the rain." They flew away.

And the rain came down: *splish splash, splish splash.*

The three butterfly brothers flew up to a beautiful white lily.

Fly up to a child who's wearing white.

"Little white lily, would you please open up your flower cup so that we can stay dry in the rain?"

Save us, save us
From the rain
Until the sun
Comes out again.

The lily said, "Butterfly White can come in because he's just like me—but not Butterfly Yellow or Butterfly Red. They are different!"

"I love my brothers," said Butterfly White. "I won't leave them out in the rain. If they can't join me, I don't want to come in either."

And the rain came down: *splish splash, splish splash.*

The sun looked down from the sky. She saw the love of the three butterfly brothers, and she wanted to help. So she pushed away the big rain cloud: push, push, push!

Hold up your hands and push, and have the children join in.

Out came the sun, big, beautiful, and warm. She dried up all the rain. Now the three butterfly brothers could fly from flower to flower to flower again. When the sun went down, the three brothers flew home.

Make flying movements in place.

This time the butterfly mother and butterfly father were waiting for them. The three butterfly brothers had a wonderful day.

Johnny Appleseed

Source:
An American folk tale, adapted.

When to tell:
- In the fall as an introduction to a unit on apples.
- As part of a lesson on ecology or the environment.
- To show the children that each of us can make a difference in helping our earth.

Suggestions:
- Bring apples to examine and eat—then plant their seeds.
- Show a picture of an apple orchard.
- Bring a U.S. map, and point out Ohio, Indiana, and Illinois—the places where Johnny Appleseed planted apple trees.
- Bring a wolf puppet to use in the story.

Johnny Appleseed

How many people here like apples? Clap your hands if you've ever been apple-picking.

Give the children time to raise their hands.

Just for a moment, let's pretend that we are in an apple orchard, and we're surrounded by rows and rows of apple trees. Reach up as high as you can, and pick one of the reddest and juiciest apples you see. Now take a bite.

With the children, gesture reaching up, picking an apple, and taking a bite. Make loud crunching sounds.

Mmm. Let's take another bite.

Apples remind me of a very special person. He was called Johnny Appleseed. Actually, his real name was Johnny Chapman. He lived a long time ago, when our country, America, was very young. He is an American folk hero, and to this day people tell stories about him.

Pause, look down at the apple, and begin the story.

People say that when Johnny Appleseed was a teeny tiny baby, just an infant in his mother's arms, he delighted in the pink and white blossoms of the apple tree. He'd point to the flowers and cry and holler until his mama broke off a blossom and handed it to him. Then he would coo and giggle and fall asleep with the blossom in his tight little fist.

Point your finger, then make a gesture of breaking off a blossom.

He was the oldest of 10 children. Imagine the noise in his house! That drove him into the forest, where it was quiet and peaceful. The animals sensed his gentleness and would join him. He'd sit under a tree, and rabbits would appear.

If your listeners are very young, you might want to count to 10 with them.

Hippity, hippity, hippity, hop,
Hippity, hippity, hop.

Squirrels would run circles around him.

Use your fingers on your knees to mimic running back and forth.

Do loo loo loo loo loo loo loo
Do loo loo loo loo loo loo loo.

And deer would peek at him from behind the trees.
Johnny knew how to care for sick animals. His granny had taught him how. He could remove thorns from paws, mend broken wings, set broken bones, and nurse sick baby animals back to health. Johnny loved the forest and the animals, but even more than those, he loved the apple tree.

He learned about apple trees from his neighbor, Mr. Smith, who had an apple orchard next to Johnny's cabin. From the time Johnny could talk, he drove poor Mr. Smith crazy with his questions! He had so much to learn.

I know that you ask a lot of questions too. Right? We all know that we learn by asking questions.

Look into the children's eyes, and give them a chance to say right.

One day when Johnny was helping Mr. Smith plant trees, he looked up at him and said, "Someday I'm going to plant apple trees all over America. The apples will feed hungry people, and the trees will make America beautiful."

Say this with conviction.

Mr. Smith smiled at Johnny and said, "Johnny Chapman, I believe you will."

That's when Johnny began to collect apple seeds.

Johnny collected seeds,
Oh, Johnny collected seeds;
Hi-ho the apple-o,
Johnny collected seeds.

During the rest of the story you'll have the opportunity to sing a series of verses to the tune of "Farmer in the Dell." Sing each verse once, and the children can repeat it with you.

Years later, when Johnny had grown into a tall

young man, he packed his belongings and put his precious seeds into a huge deerskin sack. He said goodbye to his parents and brothers and sisters and walked out the front door.

"Wait!" shouted his mama, holding a cooking pot. "What will you cook in?"

"I don't have any room for a pot," said Johnny.

His mama plopped the pot on top of his head. *Umph!* He smiled, and off he went to plant his seeds.

Johnny will plant the seeds,
Oh, Johnny will plant the seeds;
Hi-ho the apple-o,
Johnny will plant the seeds.

Johnny planted trees and made friends everywhere he went. He always had exciting adventures. Children loved Johnny because he always had stories to tell, apples to give away, and seeds to plant. One day a little girl saw him coming and shouted, "Here comes Johnny Appleseed!" The name stuck. After that everyone called him Johnny Appleseed.

There are many stories about Johnny. Let me tell you just one. One summer morning when he was walking with his sack of seeds and his pot on his head, he heard a whimpering sound. He looked down and saw a little wolf with his leg caught in a trap. Johnny loved all the animals. He wasn't afraid of the wolf, and he knew how to take care of him. He bent down, opened the trap, and gently lifted out the broken leg.

Whimper with the children.

Whimper again.

"There, there, little fella. I'll fix you up in no time. My granny taught me how."

He made a splint, bandaged the wolf's leg, and

stayed with him until he could walk on his own. Then he packed his sack full of _____.

He put his _____ (pot) on his _____ (head) and took off down the road. Johnny didn't have many belongings, and most of the time he didn't even wear shoes. In the summertime he enjoyed the *pit-pat* sound his feet made on the forest floor.

He walked away from the wolf:

Pause, and let the children fill in the correct words: apple seeds.

Pit-pat pit-pat,
Pit-pat pit-pat.

Make a rhythmic pit-pat sound with your hands on alternate knees.

He stopped for a moment and heard

Pit-pit pat-pat,
Pit-pit pat-pat.

Make the sounds again.

He walked on:

Pit-pat pit-pat,
Pit-pat pit-pat.

He heard it again:

Pit-pit pat-pat,
Pit-pit pat-pat.

He turned around, and there was the _____ (wolf). He was wagging his tail and looking up at Johnny with sorrowful eyes, as if to say, "Please take me with you."

"Well, come along," Johnny said. "There's work to be done!"

He found a wolf one day,
He found a wolf one day;
Hi-ho the apple-o,
And now he wants to stay.

Sing together.

The wolf stayed with Johnny for many, many years. He even helped him plant his seeds. The wolf would dig a hole with his front paws, and Johnny would drop in the seeds.

Make hand gestures.

As the years went by, Johnny planted trees all over Ohio, Indiana, and Illinois. Those trees gave food to the hungry families moving west. Johnny's dream was coming true!

He planted trees for a long, long time, until he was a very old man with long white hair and a long white beard.

Indicate a beard with a hand gesture from your chin.

Then one day he said, "My work is done." Johnny died under one of his beloved trees. And now it's our turn to carry on Johnny Appleseed's tradition and to plant trees. Just think: If each one of us planted a tree every year, our earth would be a better place.

Use an old, creaky voice.

We will plant a tree,
Oh, we will plant a tree;
Hi-ho the apple-o,
We will plant a tree.

The Three Billy Goats Gruff

Source:
A Norwegian folk tale, adapted.

When to tell:
- Anytime: children love this well-known story.
- To show that when we use our brains, we can overcome our enemies.

Suggestions:
- This is a perfect story for retelling with the children. Pick children to play the parts of the troll and the three billy goats while you play the narrator.
- You and the children can make simple puppets or paper-plate masks and leave them in the play area. Then the youngsters can tell the story whenever they want.

The Three Billy Goats Gruff

Once there were three billy goats gruff who were on their way to eat the green, green grass at the top of a mountain. The first was a teeny tiny billy goat, the second was a middle-sized billy goat, and the third was a great big billy goat. Together they walked toward the mountain and sang,

We are three billy goats gruff gruff gruff;
We eat till we've had enough nuff nuff.

They came to a bridge over a waterfall. Underneath the waterfall lived the meanest, ugliest, smelliest troll you can imagine. He had eyes as big as saucers and a nose as long as a broomstick.

Gesture big circles around your eyes, and with your hand indicate a long nose.

The troll was waiting for someone to cross the bridge.

The teeny tiny billy goat stepped onto the bridge. It sounded like this: *trip, trip, trip, trip.*

Make the sound with your hands on your knees, and use a very soft, small voice for the first billy goat. Use a loud, full voice for the troll.

"Who's that trip-tripping on my bridge?" asked the mean old troll.

"It is I, the teeny tiny billy goat. I'm on my way to the mountain to eat the green, green grass."

"I'll eat you whole!" said the mean old troll.

Say it once, and have the children repeat it with you.

"Don't do that," said the teeny tiny billy goat. "Another goat is on his way, and he's bigger, fatter, and more delicious."

"Be gone with you, then!" shouted the troll.

So the teeny tiny billy goat continued across the bridge: *trip, trip, trip, trip.*

Then came the middle-sized billy goat. When he

stepped onto the bridge, it sounded like this: *trip, trap, trip, trap.*

With hands on knees, make the sound somewhat louder, and use a louder voice for the middle-sized billy goat.

"Who's that trip-trapping on my bridge?" asked the mean old troll.

"It is I, the middle-sized billy goat. I'm going to the mountain to eat the green, green grass."

"I'll eat you whole!" said the mean old troll.

Have the children join in.

"Don't do that," said the middle-sized billy goat. "Another goat is right behind me, and he's bigger, fatter, and more delicious."

"Be gone with you, then!" shouted the troll.

So the middle-sized billy goat continued across the bridge: *trip, trap, trip, trap.*

Then the great big billy goat stepped onto the bridge, and it began to shake: *tramp, tramp, tramp, tramp.*

Make a louder sound, and use a loud, deep voice for the third billy goat. When he speaks, hold fingers on top of your head to indicate his horns.

"Who's that tramping on my bridge?" asked the mean old troll.

"It is I, the biggest of all the billy goats. I'm going to the mountain to eat the green, green grass."

"I'll eat you whole!" said the mean old troll.

"Come on up," said the biggest billy goat.

You think you're big;
You think you're strong.
Come on up—
I'll prove you're wrong.

The mean old troll climbed up onto the bridge. Then the great big billy goat charged at him with his horns and butted him over the edge and into the water with a loud splash. And that was the end of him.

Mime the charging.

The great big billy goat crossed the bridge: *tramp, tramp, tramp, tramp.*

The three happy billy goats went to the mountain,

where they found plenty of green, green grass. Then
they ate and ate and ate, and they sang,

We are three billy goats gruff gruff gruff;
We eat till we've had enough nuff nuff.

They ate until they were fat, like that! And that's
the end of my tale.

Puff out your cheeks, and
gesture a big stomach.

Bobbie the Boo

Source:
Inspired by "The Big Boo" from *Yetta the Trickster* (Clarion Books/Houghton Mifflin, 1976) by Andrea Griffing Zimmerman.

When to tell:
- On Halloween.
- When you have a trickster in your classroom.
- To teach that our behavior has consequences.

Suggestions:
- Teach the children to say "1, 2, 3, boo!" Practice a few times.
- Children love to participate, so pick youngsters to play the different parts. If other adults are present, put them in the story too.
- When the story is over, discuss with the children the things that scare them.

Bobbie the Boo

Bobbie was in kindergarten, and he loved school. One fine morning he got dressed and put on his soft red sneakers. He had a big smile on his face because he had a great idea.

"Good morning, Mom! Good morning, Dad!"

He ate his breakfast, grabbed his lunchbox and backpack, and went to the bus stop to wait for the bus. When he got to school, the fun began.

He saw his teacher, Miss Huggins, writing on the blackboard. He crept up behind her, counted to himself, 1, 2, 3, and said "Boo!"

"Eeek!" screamed Miss Huggins. Her chalk flew out of her hand.

Have the children say "1, 2, 3, boo!" with you.

Bobbie giggled.

"I'm sorry," he said. "I didn't mean to scare you."

Each time he giggles, you giggle—he-he-he—into your hands.

"This is fun," Bobbie said to himself. "I'll go scare Connie." Connie was Bobbie's classmate and friend. She was hanging up her coat in the big coat closet. He put a coat over his head, sneaked up behind her, and counted to himself, 1, 2, 3, "Boo!"

"Yipes!" she yelled and dropped her coat. She turned around and looked at Bobbie with an angry face. Bobbie giggled and said, "I'm sorry. I didn't mean to scare you."

About midmorning Bobbie went to the school nurse because he had a scratchy throat. Mrs. Neilson, the nurse, was taking Andrew's temperature. Bobbie hid behind the curtain until she was finished. Then he counted, 1, 2, 3, "Boo!"

She sat down quickly in the chair next to her.

Bobbie looked at her and giggled. He said, "I'm sorry. I didn't mean to scare you."

"Oh, Bobbie," said Nurse Neilson, "you scared me so. My heart is going thumpity thumpity thump!"

At lunchtime Bobbie got behind Mrs. Calabash, the cook. She was dishing out big spoonfuls of mashed potatoes. Bobbie counted to himself, 1, 2, 3, "Boo!"

Oh no! Now there were mashed potatoes everywhere! Cook Calabash looked very angry. Bobbie giggled and said, "I'm sorry. I didn't mean to scare you."

When Bobbie went to music class in the afternoon, his teacher, Mrs. Marcus, was leading the students in singing "You Are My Sunshine."

Lead the children in singing part of it: "You are my sunshine, my only sunshine," etc.

Bobbie crept up behind Mrs. Marcus and counted, 1, 2, 3, "Boo!"

"Youuu!" Mrs. Marcus sang out. Bobbie giggled and said, "I'm sorry. I didn't mean to scare you."

Let your voice rise higher.

Mrs. Marcus felt that Bobbie was being disruptive to the class, so she sent him to the office with a note to Mr. Peabody, the principal. On the way he spotted a cat that had wandered in the open door. *Meow, meow.* He followed the cat around the corner and then counted to himself, 1, 2, 3, "Boo!"

Meow with the children.

"Meow!" the cat screeched, and she ran out the door. Bobbie giggled and said, "This is fun, fun, fun!"

Say this joyfully.

But now Bobbie had to take Mrs. Marcus's note to the principal, and he was getting nervous. Mr. Peabody read the note and said, "Tomorrow when you come to school, I want you to come right to my office and sit on the bench until I come to get you."

Use a deep, stern voice.

"Yes, Mr. Peabody."

The next day Bobbie was sitting on the bench in the principal's office, wearing his soft red sneakers—just in case—when Mr. Peabody said, "Bobbie, you may go to your classroom now."

Use a stern voice.

Bobbie hurried to his kindergarten room, but . . . *no one was there!*

Teach the kids this line so they can repeat it with you.

He ran outside to the playground, but . . . *no one was there!*

He went to the nurse's office, but . . . *no one was there!*

He ran to the cafeteria, but . . . *no one was there!*

He went to the music room, but . . . *no one was there!*

"Yoo-hoo! Where is everybody?" called Bobbie. "This is creepy!"

He wandered up to the auditorium and opened the door—*creak.*

It was dark in there. All of a sudden Bobbie heard a gigantic boo!

Make sure the children join you in a loud boo.

"Oh no!" cried Bobbie, and he hid under a seat. Then the lights went on, and there was everyone from the school: the students, the teachers, the nurse, the cook, and Mr. Peabody. They all said, "We're sorry, Bobbie! We didn't mean to scare you!"

Bobbie came out from under the seat, and everyone giggled. Now Bobbie knows what it feels like when someone sneaks up and says boo!

Anansi's Good Day

Source:

An African folk tale, adapted.

When to tell:

- To show that our behavior has consequences and that being greedy gets us into trouble.
- To celebrate Black History Month.

Suggestions:

- When the story is over, you and the children can create a story about your class's good day.
- Bring in some beans, and share them after the story.
- Create a "hat-shaking dance" to music.

Anansi's Good Day

People say that all the stories about Anansi the spider come from Ghana, Africa. Anansi was the first spiderman who ever lived. He was very, very greedy, and he loved to eat.

Anansi was lazy too. Instead of planting and hunting his own food, he would use trickery to get other people's food. But every once in a while he would have a good day.* That means that the little bit of goodness deep in his heart would come bubbling up, and for one whole day he would be kind and helpful to people. Today is one of those days.

Anansi's (handwritten, above "his")

Anansi woke up with the sunlight streaming through the window of his banana-leaf house. He opened his eyes and smiled and said, "I feel great! This is one of my good days. I'll do something good for . . . let's see. I know, Granny Spider!"

He got dressed. He went into the kitchen and surprised his wife, Aso, who was cooking over the fire.

Mime putting on trousers, a shirt, and a hat.

"Aso!" he shouted. "I woke up this morning, and I said, 'I feel great!' I'm going to help Granny Spider plant her field."

Aso was delighted. She said, "Anansi, I just made a seven-layer chocolate cake. You can take it to Granny." *& remember, its not for you; its for Granny!* (handwritten)

Look down at the cake with a gleam in your eyes.

"I will," said Anansi, "but first I would like my breakfast."

Sit down, and pretend to tuck a napkin in your collar.

Anansi ate a delicious breakfast. He started with _____, and then he went on to _____ and _____ and _____.

Let the children supply the names of breakfast foods. Mimic eating them.

(handwritten margin note) * I think all people have some days when they are very good, &, sadly, some other days when they are not so good. How many of you would say that's true of you?

"That's enough!" said Anansi.

He put on his hat, picked up the cake, said goodbye to Aso, and off he went. He walked over and under rocks, through tall grass, around trees, and up the hill, and by then he was _____ (hot), and he was _____ (hungry).

So what did he do?

Not today! Remember, today is a good day. Later on, you might have to remind Anansi about ~~his~~ *this being* good day.

Finally he got to Granny's farm. "Good morning, Granny!" he said.

"Anansi, is that you? What a surprise—a cake for me. You must be having one of those good days."

"Oh yes. When I woke up this morning, I said, 'I feel great!' So ~~I've come to help you plant your seeds,~~ said Anansi. *I'll go &* "granny n her " " *on this side of my house.*

"That's wonderful. You plant ~~over there.~~ *on t other side.* I'll plant ~~over here.~~ But first I'll go into the kitchen and make a pot of Granny's famous beans."

In her pot
She took out her biggest pot and put in the beans. ~~On top of~~ the beans she *also* added _____.

Granny put on the lid and set the pot over the fire to simmer. Then she went into the field to work. *went out to help her + he*
Anansi was very good for a while. He planted seeds and sang this song: *(He liked to sing while he worked. How many of you like to sing while you work?) anansi sang:*

First ~~One,~~ dig a hole.
then ~~Two,~~ plant a seed.
all done by ~~Three~~ is a spider
Who is good indeed.

sing it w= him!

Anansi did fine until the smell of the beans came across the field and into his nose. As he worked, his

Hold your full stomach.

Gesture being hot, and let the children guess hot and hungry. Then pretend to look at the cake hungrily, and let the children guess "He ate the cake."

Use a creaky old spidery voice each time she speaks.

Gesture by pointing.

Mime the activity.

Let the children offer possible ingredients, and mime preparing and putting them in. For example, if someone suggests onions, mime cutting them and crying.

Sing or say the words. You say each sentence first, and have the children repeat after you.

40 •

planting got closer and closer to the kitchen.

First, *One*, dig a hole.
then *Two*, plant a seed.
all done by *Three is a spider*
Who is good indeed.

Say or sing the words together.

He could not resist the delicious smell of the beans. So he ran into the kitchen and took the lid off the pot.

"Oh, I know—I know it's my good day. But, I need to taste the beans for Granny to make sure they're good."

Mime lifting off the lid, and remind the children to shout, "It's your good day!"

He took the long-handled spoon and tasted the beans.

Mime tasting the beans.

"Mmm. I need another taste."

The children will yell, "No! No! It's your good day." Just ignore them.

"Mmm," said Anansi. He took off his hat, filled it with beans, and found a corner of the kitchen where he could sit and eat them. But do you think one hatful of beans is enough for a greedy spider? No! He filled up his hat a second time—and that's when it happened.

Other The farmers, who were outside working on their farms, began to sniff the air. Then they all shouted together, "Granny's famous beans!" and they ran to Granny's farm to get their share. Granny always made enough for everyone. Anansi saw them coming, and there he was with a hatful of beans.

Sniff together.

"Oh no!" said Anansi. "This is my good day, and they're going to find me with my hat full of beans."

What should he do? Finally he . . . he . . . he put his hat back on his head.

Let the children shout out some ideas.

Yipes! It was hot! The beans on his head felt hotter and hotter and hotter! Anansi began to shake his head in a funny way.

Shake your head side to side and up and down.

The farmers said, "What are you doing, Anansi?"

"What am I doing?" he said. "I know—I'm doing the hat-shaking dance!"

"Teach it to us! Teach it to us! Is this right?"

Have the children shake their heads with you.

Anansi couldn't stand it any longer. He took off his hat, and everyone laughed. He had beans everywhere.

Granny came running in and said, "Anansi, this is your good day."

Shake your head, tsk-tsk.

Anansi was so ashamed that ^(ran out into ↑ grassy fields, &) he said, "Please, tall grass, hide me."

The tall blades of grass separated so that Anansi could hide between them. And do you know something? To this day spiders hide in tall grass, and now you know why.

The Little Red House

Source:

The star in the apple, an old motif, comes from European folklore. This version of the tale was inspired by "The Little Red House With No Doors" from *Read-Aloud Stories* (Milton Bradley, 1929) by Carolyn Sherwin Bailey.

When to tell:

- In the fall.
- To teach children not to give up on a task too easily.
- Any time you need a good adventure story for young children.

Suggestions:

- Keep an apple hidden until the end of the story, when you'll cut it horizontally.
- Teach the children the following verse so they can join in throughout the story.

I'm looking for a house
Without a door,
With a star, with a star
Inside.

The Little Red House

One morning a young boy woke up and called, "Mom!"

His mother came running and said, "What's wrong?"

"I'm bored!"

"Would you like to go on an adventure?" she asked. His mom always had wonderful ideas.

His eyes got big with wonder, and he said, "Yes! Where am I going?"

"You'll be going down the lane, past the farmhouse, and up the hill."

"What for?" he asked.

"To find a little red house without a door, with a star inside," his mom answered.

"Let me see if I can remember. I'm looking for a little red _____ (house) without a _____ (door), with a _____ (star) inside."

Then he made up a song to help him remember:

I'm looking for a house
Without a door,
With a star, with a star
Inside.

His mom handed him his jacket, his hat, and his gloves because it was a cool fall day. He put on his jacket and his hat and gloves, waved goodbye to his mom, and off he went down the lane.

Cup your hands around your mouth and shout.

Gesture the directions with your hands.

See if the children can guess house and the other words.

Sing or chant the verse with the children each time it appears.

Zzzip. Mime putting on the clothing.

Each time he walks, mimic walking with your hands on your knees.

Down the lane he saw a young girl jumping rope, a-one-a-two-a-three-a-four. He said, "Excuse me."

I'm looking for a house
Without a door,
With a star, with a star
Inside.

The young girl giggled and said, "I've never heard of a house without a door. That's the silliest thing I've ever heard."

"Well, my mom told me that I'll find it, and I will," he said. He wasn't ready to give up.

"Why don't you talk to my dad?" said the young girl. "See the farm over there? My dad's the farmer painting the big red barn. He knows everything!"

"Thank you," he said, and he walked along the lane to the farmhouse. There were piles of big golden pumpkins and baskets of potatoes and yams every-where he looked.

"Well, sonny, what can I do for you?" said the farmer.

"Mr. Farmer," he said,

I'm looking for a house
Without a door,
With a star, with a star
Inside.

"I've never heard of a house without a door," said the farmer. "Did you say it had a star inside?"

"Yes," the boy said, and a big tear rolled down his cheek. "I don't know if I'll ever find it. My mom sent me out on this adventure, but I'm not having any fun.

I'm not ready to give up, though."

"Well, sonny," the farmer said, "you need to talk to Granny. She's old and wise. She lives at the bottom of the hill, and she knows everything."

He picked himself up, waved goodbye, and off he went. There Granny was, sitting in a creaky old rocking chair at the bottom of the hill.

Wave.

Mimic the sounds of the chair moving back and forth: err-eee, err-eee.

"Are you Granny?"

"Sure, I'm Granny! Who else would I be, young whippersnapper?"

Use a funny creaky voice each time she speaks.

"Granny," said the young boy, "I hope you can help me."

I'm looking for a house
Without a door,
With a star, with a star
Inside.

"Hey," said Granny, "I wouldn't mind having a house without a door. It'd be nice in the wintertime—the cold air wouldn't come in. And if I had a star inside, I'd knit and read all night!"

"Do you know where I can find one?" he asked. "I'm tired and hungry. But I'm not ready to give up yet!"

"Can't say that I do," Granny said. "Why don't you walk up the hill and talk to the wind? He whips around people's chimneys at night and listens. The wind knows everything."

"Thanks, Granny. I'll go see the wind."

"Good luck, you little whippersnapper."

He began to walk up the hill, and he heard the wind: *whooo.*

You and the children make wind sounds.

"Mr. Wind, is that you?"

"Whaaat dooo youuu waaant?" said the wind.

The young boy answered,

I'm looking for a house
Without a door,
With a star, with a star
Inside.

"Follow meee!" said the wind.

He followed the wind and went up, up, up the hill, faster and faster and faster.

Make your hand and knee gestures comically faster and faster.

When he got to the top of the hill, he was in an apple orchard. "Oh, Mr. Wind, could you blow me down one of those juicy ripe red apples?"

Blow like the wind.

Plop! A big red juicy apple fell in front of him. When he picked it up and opened his mouth to take a bite, the wind blew in his ear. The wind whispered that the apple-blossom queen lives in the apple and that the stem is her chimney.

Blow like the wind.

The boy looked down at his apple and said, "Could this be the little red house without a door, with a star inside? I think it is! Thank you, Mr. Wind!"

He ran down the hill, past Granny rocking in her chair, past the farmhouse, down the lane, past the young girl jumping rope, and all the way home.

Instead of walking with your hands, now move them rapidly to indicate running.

He knocked on the door of his house: *knock, knock.*

His mom came to the door and said, "Welcome back. Did you find it?"

"Yes! It's an apple!" He handed her the apple.

Take your apple out of hiding, and cut it horizontally.

"That's right!" she said. "Now let me show you something."

She took the apple and cut it in half in a very special way. And inside . . . was a star!

"You see," she said, "The apple-blossom queen

Pause, and speak in a hushed voice. Then show the halves of the apple.

48 •

lives in every single apple."

So when you go home tonight, if you have an apple in your house, ask your mom or dad to cut it open for you. Then you can see the star too.

The Grasshopper and the Ant

Source:
Aesop's Fables, adapted.

When to tell:
- To introduce the seasons.
- To reinforce good work habits.
- To show that our behavior has consequences.
- To lead into a discussion of friendship.

Suggestions:
- Show pictures of summer insects.
- After the story you and the listeners can sing and dance like Gussie Grasshopper. Put on music or repeat the story's songs.
- Ask the children what they like to do once they've finished their chores. (Example: After I help to set the table, Mom reads me a book.)

The Grasshopper and the Ant

Gussie Grasshopper *felt like she* was the happiest of creatures. He loved to leap, hop, sing, and dance.

"I love the summer!" Gussie would say. "I can sing and dance all day, and I can sing and dance all night." Crowds would gather around Gussie Grasshopper just to watch him perform.

Say this with enthusiasm.

I sing and dance at every chance
(Clap, clap, clap, clap)
Deep in the heart of summer.
Come, everyone, and join the fun
(Clap, clap, clap, clap)
Deep in the heart of summer.

This verse is sung to the tune of "Deep in the Heart of Texas." Teach it to the children so you can sing together.

In the early *spring* summer, insect eggs hatch, and butter- *caterpillars* flies emerge from their cocoons *as beautiful butterflies*. It's a time of new beginnings. If you listen quietly on a warm summer night, you can hear the celebration *all nature*—the mosquitoes buzzing, the cicadas singing. And you can watch the lightning bugs lighting up the night. All summer long they can be seen and heard. But when the air turns cool, and fall is in the air, the insects begin to get ready for the cold silent winter.

But not Gussie Grasshopper. He continued to go out in the field every day to sing and dance.

I sing and dance at every chance
(Clap, clap, clap, clap)
Deep in the heart of summer.
Come, everyone, and join the fun

• 53

(Clap, clap, clap, clap)
Deep in the heart of summer.

But now he was all alone.

One day Audrey Ant came by. Audrey was dragging along a large kernel of corn.

"Hello, Gussie," she said. "You look like you're having fun. I wish I could join you."

Look sad and forlorn.

"Well, come on—sing and dance with me."

Gesture with your hands.

Come sing and dance the whole day long;
Come sing away your sorrow.
Come sing and dance the whole day long;
We'll worry about food tomorrow.

Sing this verse to the tune of "Pop Goes the Weasel." Sing it once, and have the children join in.

"Come join me, Audrey Ant," said Gussie. "You're not having any fun. Life's too short!"

Make welcoming gestures.

"I'm gathering my food for the winter," she said. "The days are turning cool, and winter will soon be here."

"Winter?" asked Gussie. "You're not worried about winter now, are you? The sun is still warm; we have plenty of food."

Come sing and dance the whole day long;
Come sing away your sorrow.
Come sing and dance the whole day long;
We'll worry about food tomorrow.

You and the children sing together.

So for a little while Audrey sang and danced with Gussie and had a wonderful time.

"I can't stay," said Audrey Ant. "I have work to do. Perhaps when I finish, I'll be back."

"Don't work too hard!" Gussie said. "Just think

Pick a child from the audience to sing and dance with you. Repeat the verse one more time.

about me having a great time!"

Throughout the fall Gussie Grasshopper played while Audrey Ant worked. Then winter came, with its ice, snow, and cold winds. Gussie was s-o-o-o *cold* and s-o-o-o *hungry*.

Shiver with the children.

One cold winter's day Audrey was dragging out some grains of food to dry in the sun. Gussie Grasshopper hopped over and said, "Hello, A-u-d-r-e-e-e-y. Do you r-e-m-e-m-b-e-r-r-r me?"

Shiver.

"Sure I do!" she answered. "You're the one who sang and danced all summer and fall."

Gussie said, "And now I'm hungry. It's s-o-o-o *cold*, and I have nothing to eat. Will you share some of your food with me? Please?"

Shiver, and look forlorn and sad.

Audrey looked at Gussie and said, "Why should I? You played while I worked. I dragged every one of these heavy pieces of grain myself while you were singing and dancing."

Gussie looked so unhappy and so cold, and he said, "I know I've been very foolish. Now I know that I should work before I play. But . . . I have nothing to eat. I will surely die."

Say this line slowly.

Audrey Ant looked at Gussie Grasshopper, and she knew he had learned his lesson. "All right," she said, "I will share with you. But next year you must gather your own food."

"I will! I promise," said Gussie.

Audrey shared with Gussie all winter long. And as far as I know, since that time Gussie Grasshopper and Audrey Ant have been the best of friends.

Why Bear Sleeps All Winter Long

Source:

Adapted from a Native American story I heard as a child.

When to tell:

- In wintertime.
- To lead to a discussion of what animals do in the winter.
- To show the children that sometimes we need our friends to help us solve our problems.

Suggestions:

- Divide the children into two groups. One group will be rabbits; the other, bears. Teach the rabbits the following chant:

Help me, help me,
Stop Brown Bear.
He's tricking me;
It is not fair.

- Practice the following activities with the bears:
  A) Eat like bears—pretend to use your paws to grab food, shove it in your mouth noisily, and say, "Yum, yum, yum."
  B) Make a snoring sound: *zzzzz*.
  C) Yawn loudly—*Aahhch*—using big arm movements.

■ Teach all the children the following chant:

Brown Bear, Brown Bear,
He's the one
Who's tricking Rabbit
Just for fun.

■ Try turning this story into a puppet show. To do so, you'll need puppets
  for Rabbit, Bear, Frog, Squirrel, Mole, and Fox, which you and the children
  can make simply from bags or paper plates.
■ Consider making the story into a play for parents' day. The main
  characters can wear special noses or ears. The children in the chorus can
  be forest trees chanting the verses.
■ Show pictures of the winter forest, explaining how animals cope
  with cold weather.

Why Bear Sleeps All Winter Long

Rabbit was a serious, hard-working animal. She never bothered any of the other animals. She was always busy!

In the fall she was busier than ever, gathering her acorns. Sometimes she went with Fox to the farm. Fox looked after the chickens, and Rabbit picked cabbages, pulled up turnips and carrots, and then stored them for the cold winter days to come. She was very generous; she often shared her food with the field mice and chipmunks.

And then there was Bear. He filled his days with gathering wild honey and fishing and sleeping in the warm sun. But Bear still found time for mischief. He loved to play tricks on the other animals, especially Rabbit.

For example: Just as soon as Rabbit filled her tree stump with fall vegetables, along came Bear. He scooped up all the vegetables and carried them off.

Brown Bear, Brown Bear,
He's the one
Who's tricking Rabbit
Just for fun.

Just as soon as Rabbit filled her stump with warm dry leaves for winter, along came Bear! He stomped through the leaves and scattered them everywhere.

Bears eat honey—yum, yum, yum!

Bears grab fish—yum, yum, yum!

Bears snore: zzzzz.

Rabbits gesture putting fall vegetables in a stump. Then bears gesture scooping up the vegetables.

Everyone chants.

Bears stand up and stomp in place.

• 59

Brown Bear, Brown Bear,
He's the one
Who's tricking Rabbit
Just for fun.

As soon as Rabbit found a special place to hide her nuts, along came Bear! He found the nuts and threw them out.

Bears gesture throwing nuts.

Brown Bear, Brown Bear,
He's the one
Who's tricking Rabbit
Just for fun.

Rabbit couldn't take any more of Bear's tricks. She didn't know what to do.

Finally she said, "I can't keep Bear away by myself. I'll go ask my friends for help." And she hopped over to the pond to find Frog. She called out, "Frog, Frog . . ."

Help me, help me,
Stop Brown Bear.
He's tricking me;
It is not fair!

Rabbits chant this verse each time it appears.

Frog said, "Let's go see Squirrel. Maybe she can help." So Frog and Rabbit went to see Squirrel, who was busy cracking nuts in a hickory tree. Frog said, "Squirrel, Squirrel, Rabbit needs your help!"

Help me, help me,
Stop Brown Bear.
He's tricking me;
It is not fair!

Squirrel dropped her nuts and said, "Let's go see Mole. Maybe he can help. Follow me."

So Squirrel and Frog and Rabbit went to find Mole. Mole was digging a new home for himself, and dirt was flying out of the hole as he dug. Squirrel and Frog said, "Mole, Mole, Rabbit needs your help!"

Help me, help me,
Stop Brown Bear.
He's tricking me;
It is not fair!

Mole said, "Let's go find Fox. He's the clever one—he'll think of some way to stop Bear. Follow me."

So Mole, Squirrel, Frog, and Rabbit went to find Fox. They found him behind a bush, grooming his bushy tail.

Mole and Squirrel and Frog said, "Fox, Fox, Rabbit needs your help!"

Help me, help me,
Stop Brown Bear.
He's tricking me;
It is not fair!

"Hmm," said Fox. "Let me think. Has anyone seen Bear today?"

"Not me," said Rabbit.

"Not me," said Frog.

"Not me," said Squirrel.

"Not me," said Mole.

"Let's go find him," said Fox.

The animals followed Fox. They looked here, they looked there, they looked everywhere!

"Here he is!" said Fox at last. Bear was asleep in a hollow log: zzzzz.

Bears snore.

"Now I know what to do," said Fox. "Frog, bring me some mud from your pond. Squirrel, bring me some leaves from your tree. Mole, bring me some of your digging dirt—and hurry!"

The animals went their separate ways. Bear was still asleep: zzzzz.

Bears snore.

They returned quickly, and Fox said, "Rabbit, fill up Bear's log with mud from Frog's pond, leaves from Squirrel's tree, and dirt from Mole's new hole."

Rabbit filled up the log, and then she used her hind legs to pack the mud, leaves, and dirt in tightly.

Thud, thud, thud!

Lead the rabbits, making a thudding sound with hands on knees and saying thud, thud, thud!

Then the animals left Bear to sleep: zzzzz. Bear slept and slept and slept! Each time he woke up, he saw that it was still dark. *What a long night*, thought Bear as he fell back to sleep.

Bears snore.

He slept all winter long, and when he finally woke up, he felt great. He was very rested.

Lead the bears in a huge yawn.

He pushed the mud and leaves and dirt out of the log and saw that it was spring. The birds were singing, the sun was shining, the wildflowers were in bloom. And Bear said, "I slept all winter. I shall do this every year!"

Use a deep, bearlike voice.

Rabbit was very pleased. After that she always had a peaceful winter. She even found time to dance and play in the snow.

So now you know why Bear sleeps all winter long.

The Gossipy Child

Source:
A Jewish folk tale, adapted.

When to tell:
When children say unkind things to one another.

Suggestions:
■ Teach the following verse, sung to the tune of "You Are My Sunshine":

You are a gossip, a mean old gossip.
You make us feel bad with unkind words.
Don't ever lie again
Or make us cry again.
Then we'll be proud
To call you a friend.

■ Ask the children whether they understand what the word *gossip* means. You might ask, "Has anyone ever said something hurtful to you? Perhaps someone has called you crybaby or dummy or fatso. How did that make you feel?"

The Gossipy Child

At home Harold was a wonderful child—just like you!

He would try all the food put in front of him—just like you!

He would put away his toys at night—just like you!

He would help out around the house—just like you!

At the end of each sentence, have the children join in with "just like you!" Then you may continue with suggestions from the children.

But when Harold was in school, he had a problem—a big problem. He was a gossip. He said unkind and hurtful things about the other children in his class.

"Clara couldn't answer the teacher's question. Tee-he-he."

"Jimmy cried yesterday on the playground. He's a crybaby!"

Move around the room from child to child as you say these gossipy words, using a stage whisper.

"Johnny smells bad. P.U.!"

Hold your nose.

"Nobody picked Melissa to be on their team. She had tears in her eyes. Tee-he-he."

Harold made a lot of the children in Mrs. Goldberg's class cry.

If you're
You are a gossip, a mean old gossip,
You make us feel bad with unkind words.
So Don't ever lie again
Or make us cry again.
Then we'll be proud
To call you a friend.

Sing this song with the children to the tune of "You Are My Sunshine."

But Harold kept on making fun of his classmates.

One day, when Harold was home sick with the chickenpox, the children complained to Mrs. Goldberg about him.

"Good morning, children."

Use a teacherlike voice.

"Good morning, Mrs. Goldberg."

Have the children say this together.

"Does anyone have anything special to tell us before we begin our day's work?"

"I do," said Jeremy. "It's about Harold. He says mean things to us. Yesterday he told Lizzy that her new dress was ugly and that she looked like an old lady. And he laughed at my picture—he said I scribbled like a baby."

"Yeah," said Trish, "he said my new haircut made me look like a boy!" Trish's eyes filled with tears. "He told Chrissy that her letter *d*'s were backward and said that means she's dumb."

The children went on and on with their complaints.

If you're
~~You are~~ a gossip, a mean old gossip,
You make us feel bad with unkind words.
So ~~Don't~~ ever lie again
Or make us cry again.
Then we'll be proud
To call you a friend.

Sing with the children.

"Hmm. Is that so? He said all that?" Mrs. Goldberg looked very thoughtful, and she said, "When Harold comes back to school, I'll talk to him."

A week later Harold returned, looking miserable, with red dots all over his face and body. Mrs. Goldberg asked him to stay after school that day.

"Harold," she said, "I'm happy to see you back in school. I hope you're feeling better. While you were gone, the children told me about your gossiping. They say you're unkind to them."

Use your teacher voice.

"Oh, that," said Harold. "I'm just having a little

fun. Those are just words . . . I can take them back anytime I want."

"Harold," said Mrs. Goldberg, "I want you to do something for me."

"Sure, Mrs. Goldberg," said Harold. He really liked his teacher and wanted to please her.

"Good! Take this pillow filled with feathers." Mrs. Goldberg picked up one of the pillows from the reading center. "Now go outside on the playground, and shake it until all the feathers have scattered. It's a windy day, so you should have lots of fun."

When Harold got to the playground, some of his classmates were already happily playing. He shook the pillow, and the feathers flew everywhere. The children chased the feathers and had a wonderful time.

Pretend to shake a pillow. The children can pretend to catch the feathers, and you can make wind sounds.

Harold went back inside the school with the empty pillowcase. "And now, Harold," said Mrs. Goldberg, "here's a basket. Collect the feathers, and bring them back to me."

"But I can't!" he protested. "The wind blew them away!"

Harold went outside with the basket, but he only found a few feathers. When he came back into the classroom, Mrs. Goldberg looked in the basket and said, "Once you released the feathers, they scattered, and you couldn't gather them back **again**."

"Yes, Mrs. Goldberg."

"Your unkind, gossipy words are the same as the feathers. Once you've spoken them, they have a life of their own and cannot be taken back. Remember that, Harold, and from now on, think very carefully before you say anything unkind to anyone."

You are a gossip, a mean old gossip.
You make us feel bad with unkind words.
Don't ever lie again
Or make us cry again.
Then we'll be proud
To call you a friend.

Repeat the song once more.

The Boy Who Became a Caribou

Source:

An Eskimo folk tale, adapted.

When to tell:

- On a cold winter's day.
- To show how hurtful name-calling can be.
- To introduce Alaska and its special climate and animals.

Suggestions:

- Locate Alaska on a U.S. map.
- Show pictures of an Eskimo, the tundra, a caribou, and/or a ptarmigan.
- Because some of the story's references will probably be new to the students, you may wish to use the following brief introduction:

This is an Eskimo story from Alaska. The Eskimo village in the story is along the Seward Peninsula, where it is very, very cold most of the year. Many Eskimos live on the tundra, which is flat land without trees, where it snows and snows and snows. The Eskimo boys and men are hunters. They hunt and fish so that the people in the village have food to eat. The girls and women clean the fish and animals and then dry them or store them or cook them. The girls and women also sew the animal skins into clothes and blankets. All the Eskimo people work very hard.

The Boy Who Became a Caribou

Long, long ago there was an Eskimo boy who was not a very good hunter. He was very unhappy. Tears would roll down his cheeks, and the other boys would sing:

Crybaby, crybaby,
Boo hoo hoo.
You can't catch a caribou.

Say it once, and let the children chant it with you.

He was so miserable that he decided to leave his igloo home and journey out into the tundra. He said goodbye to his parents and his two brothers, put on his warmest clothes, took some dried meat and fish, and off he went.

Since the tundra was covered with snow, his boots made a crunching sound as he walked: *crunch, crunch, crunch.*

He saw a flock of beautiful ptarmigans—birds that are as white as snow in the wintertime and brown in the spring and summer. He watched as they found berries to eat and flew happily in the sunshine.

"That's what I want to be," he said, "a ptarmigan!"

Say this with great enthusiasm.

He walked toward the birds: *crunch, crunch, crunch.*

They saw him coming and lifted up their wings. They looked like a white cloud lifting off the ground, and they flew away from the Eskimo boy.

Lift up your arms, and have the children join you. Then flap, and have the children flap too.

Crunch, crunch, crunch. Each time he got close to them, they would fly away. Finally at day's end he caught up with them and said, "Do not be afraid; I do not want to hurt you. I want to be just like you. I want

Repeat flying movement.

to be a ptarmigan!"

"But why? You are a fine boy," said the oldest and wisest of the birds.

"I am unhappy as a boy," he said. "I am not a skilled hunter, and the other boys make fun of me."

"A ptarmigan does not have an easy life either. We are hunted by other birds, animals, and people."

The young boy said,

I do believe that you are right,
But could I please just spend the night?

The birds gave him a white sheepskin to sleep on and a brown sheepskin to use as a cover. He was warm and snug all night, but when he woke up the next day, he was s-s-h-h-i-v-v-e-r-r-i-n-g! The birds were gone, and so were the sheepskins. But he saw a brown and a white feather on the snow. *Shiver together.*

The boy began his journey again, walking across the snowy tundra: *crunch, crunch, crunch.*

He spotted two rabbits playing happily among the willows, and he watched them eat and play. "That's what I want to be—a rabbit!" he shouted.

He walked toward the rabbits: *crunch, crunch, crunch.* *Repeat the crunching and the hopping sounds.*

The rabbits hopped away: *hoppity, hoppity, hop, hop, hop.*

"Wait!" he said. "I do not want to hurt you. I want to be a rabbit too. I don't like being a boy. I'm not a very good hunter, and the other children make fun of me."

Crybaby, crybaby, *Have the children join in.*
Boo hoo hoo.
You can't catch a caribou.

"You will not be happy as a rabbit," the rabbits said. "Large birds hunt us from the air, foxes and wolves lie in wait, and the minks and weasels take our babies."

The boy said,

I do believe that you are right,
But could I please just spend the night?

The rabbits gave him a white fur sleeping bag. All night he was snug and warm. But when he woke up, he was s-s-h-h-i-v-v-e-r-r-i-n-g! The rabbits were gone, and so was the sleeping bag. In its place was a ball of rabbit fur.

And so he set out again: *crunch, crunch, crunch.*

He saw a herd of caribou grazing on a hillside. They looked fat and content.

"That's what I want to be—a caribou!" he said. He walked toward the herd: *crunch, crunch, crunch.*

The caribou ran away.

The boy kept following them: *crunch, crunch, crunch.*

And the herd kept running away from him.

He finally caught up with them at day's end. "Caribou," he said, "I do not want to harm you. I want to be just like you. I want to be a caribou!"

"Why?" asked the chief of the herd.

The Eskimo boy explained how unhappy he was, and the caribou listened. Then the chief said, "We have decided to let you become one of us. As you sleep tonight, your body will be transformed into the body of a caribou."

That night as he slept, antlers grew from his head, and four legs with hooves grew from his body. Fur

Using your feet, make a thundering sound. Have the children join you.

Make the thundering sound.

Gesture to indicate the growth of the antlers and legs.

began to grow from his skin.

In the morning he was a caribou! At first the antlers felt heavy, and his back hurt, and he had to get used to eating the moss that grows under the snow. Then he began to enjoy himself. He learned the ways of the caribou, and he was happy.

But one morning he woke up missing his parents and brothers. The chief said, "It is time for you to go back to your people. Leave with my blessing."

So he said goodbye to his caribou friends and walked toward his village. Along the way two young hunters spotted him and said, "Look, a caribou walking toward our village!"

"Wait! Do not kill me," he said. "Just remove the skin from my head, and you will see who I am."

"Our brother!" they shouted. "You're back!"

The Eskimo boy emerged from the caribou skin and hugged his brothers. When the three of them got home, his parents were very pleased to see him. His mother couldn't believe her eyes.

He looked up into his mother's face and said, "I'm so happy to be back. I'm happy to be myself again!"

The boys in the village were sorry for what they had done, and they told him so: "We're sorry! We're glad you're back. We'll teach you to be a good hunter."

So from them he learned how to be a good hunter, and from him they learned the ways of the caribou. From that day on, the Eskimo boy was happy being himself.

The North Wind and the Sun

Source:
Jean de la Fontaine's *Fables*, adapted.

When to tell:
- When talking about weather.
- To introduce the spring.
- For a discussion of bullies and the virtue of gentleness.

Suggestions:
- Teach the following verses for the sun and the north wind before telling the story.

Sun:
I am the sun, so warm and bright;
I shine and shine until it's night.

Wind:
I am the wind, as you can see;
I blow cold, icy air with glee.

- After you've told the story, enlist the children's help in telling it again. Split the children into two groups to chant the parts of the sun and the north wind. Take the part of the narrator, and select youngsters to play the mother and the young girl.

The North Wind and the Sun

Most of the time the north wind and the sun were very good friends. The wind would visit the sun and tell her about his adventures. He went many places and knew many things. Sun was a good listener and thought Wind was strong and powerful.

But one day the north wind began to brag. "Sun, have you ever thought of how strong I am?" he said. "When I blow my cold, icy breath, things happen."

Ask your listeners "What does happen?" Add two or three responses to the story. Do the same with the sun.

I am the wind, as you can see;
I blow cold, icy air with glee.

"But I'm strong too, Wind," said Sun, "just different. When I shine, things happen too!"

I am the sun, so warm and bright;
I shine and shine until it's night.

At that moment a young girl was getting ready to step outside. It was a beautiful spring day, and she had a new red jacket to wear. Red was her favorite color, and she could zip the jacket herself.

Zzzip

"Mom, I'm going out to play. I *love* my new spring jacket."

Her mom had tied red ribbons on her braids to match her jacket, and she was so proud of her new outfit. "Play in the front yard," her mom said. "I'll call you when lunch is ready."

The young girl stepped outside with her bouncing ball and started playing.

The north wind and the sun watched as the young girl walked out of her house. The wind said, "I know what we can do: we can have a contest to see who is stronger. See the young girl with the red jacket? Whoever can get her to take off her jacket wins."

"I'm ready," said the sun.

"Good," said North Wind. "I'll go first. Watch me win this contest with all my blustery strength. Here goes!"

Pantomime throwing the ball in the air and catching it. Throw the pretend ball to a child in the audience, and ask him or her to throw it back. This is a wonderful way to include very shy children in the story.

I am the wind, as you can see;
I blow cold, icy air with glee.

The north wind blew with all of his strength. *Whoosh! Whoosh!*

The leaves blew off the trees, the flowers bent their heads to the ground, frightened animals ran for cover, and umbrellas and hats flew through the air.

The young girl lost her ball, and her ribbons flew off her braids. She shivered and ran toward her house.

"My turn," said Sun. "Just look at what your windy strength has done. That young girl is clinging to her jacket."

Wave your arms back and forth, and make wind sounds; ask the children to join you.

I am the sun, so warm and bright;
I shine and shine until it's night.

Then the sun sent her warm, gentle rays down to the earth, and everything became calm. The birds began to sing, the trees grew very still, the flowers raised their heads, and the animals peeked out of their hiding places. The young girl took off her gloves and decided to stay outside and play.

Make a circle with your hands above your head, and move your arms down slowly.

The sunshine grew warmer. She unzipped her *Zzzip*
jacket, took it off, put it down carefully in the grass,
and continued to play. She chased the butterflies,
smelled the flowers, and enjoyed the warm spring day.

The contest was over. The sun's warm, gentle
strength had won. The north wind learned his lesson.

"You are right, Sun," he said. "You are important
too. I see that you can get things done with gentleness." And to this day the north wind and the sun are
very good friends.

Gentleness, gentleness, gentleness won.
Gentleness gets many things done.

The Farmer
And the Spiderweaver

Source:

A Japanese folk tale. Inspired by the version "The Spider Weaver" from *Little One-Inch and Other Japanese Children's Favorite Stories* (Charles E. Tuttle, 1958), edited by Florence Sakade.

When to tell:

- To introduce a unit on Japan, spiders, or weather.
- To show the children that one good deed deserves another.

Suggestions:

- Use Japanese music from the library to set the mood. Have the children close their eyes and visualize, and ask them to tell you what they see.
- Show the children where Japan is on a map.
- Show pictures of spiders and webs.
- Show pictures of kimonos, or bring one to show if possible.
- Take the children outside, and ask them to look up at the clouds and tell you what shapes they see.
- Teach the children the following verse so they can sing it with you throughout the story.

Weaving is what spiders do,
And so I'll weave the whole day through.

The Farmer And the Spiderweaver

In long ago Japan, in the time of mysteries, there lived a young farmer. Every day he would work in his fields from sunup to sundown.

Gesture with your arms the sun's going up and down. Ask the children to join in.

One morning he saw a snake—*tssst*—slithering through the grass. He watched as the snake got ready to strike at a spider. The farmer took his hoe and chased away the snake.

Make a slithering sound, and indicate the snake's creeping side-to-side motion with your hands, palms together.

The spider was safe! Before it disappeared in the tall grass, it looked as if it were bowing to the farmer. He bowed back and quickly returned to his work.

The next day, just as the sun was coming up, the farmer heard singing outside his window. He looked out and saw a beautiful young woman with long shiny black hair and wearing a colorful cotton kimono. She said, "Young farmer, I have come to weave for you."

Gesture slowly.

> *Please, good farmer,*
> *Let me stay.*
> *I'll weave for you*
> *Every day.*

Each time she speaks, put your palms together, bow your head, and speak in a soft voice.

The farmer was very pleased, and he led her to the weaving room. There she would sleep and weave until her work was done. She sat down at the loom, and the farmer went into his fields to work.

When the sun went down, the farmer hurried home and knocked gently on the door of the weaving room:

Gesture slowly.

knock, knock.

"Young farmer, you may enter."

What a surprise! She had woven enough cloth to make many kimonos.

Show excitement.

"How did you weave so quickly?" asked the astonished farmer.

She raised her eyes to his and said, "Never, never ask me questions, and do not watch me as I weave or else I must leave."

He quickly agreed. Every day he would work in the fields, and every evening he would knock on her door: *knock, knock.* She would say, "Young farmer, you may enter."

Every day she wove piles of cloth. On weekends the farmer took some of the beautifully woven cloth to the market to sell. He was becoming a rich man. He felt very lucky indeed.

But then one day he forgot to take his lunch with him into the fields, so he walked back home to get it. He passed the window of the weaving room, and he could not resist peeking in.

He could not believe his eyes! Instead of a beautiful young woman, he saw a spider, weaving with her eight legs. The thread was coming from her mouth, and she was singing softly:

Weaving is what spiders do,
And so I'll weave the whole day through.

Sing to the tune of "Twinkle, Twinkle, Little Star."

He recognized her as the very same spider he had saved from the snake. She had transformed herself into a young woman so that she could weave for him.

He never said a word to her about what he had seen, and when he got back to his fields that day, he sang to himself:

Weaving is what spiders do,
And so I'll weave the whole day through.

Have the children join you.

All went well—until one evening his luck changed. He knocked on her door: *knock, knock.*

"Young farmer, you may enter. I am happy to see you, and I must tell you that I have run out of the cotton thread I weave into cloth."

"You have woven beautiful cloth for me," said the farmer. "I am very grateful. Tomorrow I will go into the village and buy more thread."

He started out early, before the sun was up. He walked across his fields and into the village. It took him all morning to get there and buy enough thread to fill his empty sack. On the way back, his bundle grew heavy, and the sun was hot. So he rested under a shady tree, and he fell asleep.

Then something terrible happened. Remember the snake? Well, there he was—*tssst*—and he crawled into the farmer's sack and coiled up at the bottom. When the farmer woke up, it was late. He picked up his sack and walked home. Then he knocked on the weaver's door: *knock, knock.*

Make the slithering sound and motion along with the children.

"Young farmer, you may enter."

She took the sack and set it on the floor next to the weaving room. As soon as the farmer left, she sat down and began to eat the cotton thread so she could weave in the morning. She had eaten her fill when she heard a slithering sound—*tssst*—and saw the snake!

He chased her around the room. She crawled up to the window and fell into the tall grass. She was moving slowly because she was full of cotton. The snake moved quickly and almost caught her.

At that moment the friendly moon looked down from the sky and saw what was happening. The moon knew that this was the good spider who had been weaving her thanks to the farmer. So the moon sent down a silvery moonbeam. The spider crawled up the moonbeam into the sky, and she was safe!

With a hand gesture, indicate the moonbeam's coming down and the spider's crawling up.

She was so full of cotton that she began to weave soft, cottony, fluffy, white clouds for the moon.

"Oh, thank you, Moon!" she said. "I'll always make you clouds!"

From that day forth the spider has woven clouds for the moon. Have you seen them? Look up in the sky, and you will.

Weaving is what spiders do,
And so I'll weave the whole day through.